CURLING SECRETS

How to Think & Play Like a Pro

COLLEEN JONES

NIMBUS
PUBLISHING

Nimbus Publishing Limited
PO Box 9166, Halifax, NS B3K 5M8
(902) 455-4286 www.nimbus.ns.ca

Printed and bound in Canada

Cover design: Heather Bryan
Interior design: Melissa Townsend
Author photo: Andrew Macnaughton

Library and Archives Canada Cataloguing in Publication

Jones, Colleen, 1959-
Curling secrets : how to think and play
like a pro / Colleen Jones.

ISBN 978-1-55109-634-6
ISBN-10 1-55109-634-X

1. Curling. I. Title.

GV845.J66 2007   796.964   C2007-904885-4

We acknowledge the financial support of the Government of Canada through the Book Publishing Industry Development Program (BPIDP) and the Canada Council, and of the Province of Nova Scotia through the Department of Tourism, Culture and Heritage for our publishing activities.

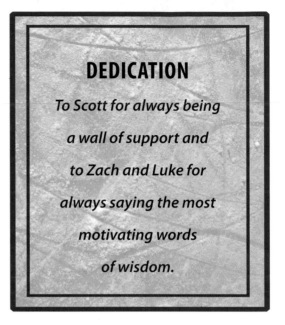

DEDICATION

To Scott for always being

a wall of support and

to Zach and Luke for

always saying the most

motivating words

of wisdom.

Photo Credits

(All numbers below refer to page numbers.)

Mike Burns Sr. and Scott Paper/Kruger Inc.: vii.

Paul Darrow: 17, 47, 49, 69.

Andrew Klaver and Scott Paper/Kruger Inc.:
23, 25, 27, 29, 30, 33, 34, 43, 44, 45, 54, 56, 57, 61, 70, 84.

Tim Krochak: 5, 15, 18, 19, 20, 21, 22, 38, 39, 40, 41.

CONTENTS

INTRODUCTION

I started curling when I was fourteen. It was a rite of passage in our house. I followed my big sisters, Barbara, Maureen, and Sheila, to the Mayflower Curling Club and started playing. When I wasn't on the ice, I practised my slide in sock feet on the kitchen floor. Back in the seventies when I started, we swept with corn brooms, so my sisters and I would go down to the furnace room and practice our sweeping until our parents grew tired of the thumping noise and yelled down for us to stop the racket. It was a humble start.

What I knew right away was that I simply loved the game, and from the very beginning I was looking for ways to get better. If you want to become a champion, this is the number one ingredient you need—passion for the game. Curling will frustrate the hell out of you along the way, but only temporarily if you love it. You'll see the frustrations, tough losses, and slumps as part of the journey to making you a better curler—that is, as long as you're willing to learn from those tough times. I remember playing in the Canada Winter Games trials when I was fifteen years old and losing a game so badly (13–2, I think) that I left out the back door of the club and cried the whole walk home. After I got over what seemed to me at the time the most devastating, earth-shattering loss of my life, I started trying to figure out where I went wrong. The answer was obvious. I missed too much. The solution was easy. Start practising. At the time of my 13–2 loss, I was just a Saturday-morning-league curler who played in a few bonspiels. I expected to get better just by showing up. The expression "practice makes perfect" became a tried-and-true expression for a reason—it's true.

Kim Kelly, Mary Anne Arsenault, Nancy Delahunt, and I put together a winning streak that saw us capture four Canadian women's championships in a row (five overall), as well as two world titles, all in a span of six years. It was a special run. No one had ever achieved that level of extended success in women's curling and the big catch to it all was that no one with half a brain would have picked our team to be so successful. We were the most unassuming, unspectactular, just-fell-off-the-turnip-truck (Nancy's favourite expression to describe us) team going. Yet we were remarkably successful. How did we do it? I'm letting the secrets out of the bag in this book. If you follow some of my suggestions, I'm sure you'll see improvements in your game. If you follow all of them, the sky's the limit. My message to you is simple: If we can win, anyone can.

Just don't expect to snap your fingers and have it happen. Success does take a lot of hard work, but I'll show you the steps my team took that made us tough to beat.

When curling became a fully recognized Olympic sport at the 1998 Games, it changed the focus for many curlers. Before 1998, the goal for the best players was to win the Canadian championship and then to win the world championship. All of that has changed with the opportunity to curl at the Olympics.

The 1982 Canadian women's curling champions. From left: Kay Zinck, Colleen Jones, Monica Jones-Moriarty, Barbara Jones-Gordon.

Recently on one of our *CBC News: Morning* shows, music giant David Foster was our guest after being inducted into the Canadian Music Hall of Fame. Our anchor, Heather Hiscox, asked him what it took to be successful in the music industry. He said, "Talent plus energy equals success." His quote spoke to me because while it's true in just about every field, it's especially true in sports. It's not enough to have talent—there are thousands of curlers in Canada with a lot of talent. It's the energy part of the equation that is the intangible in winning.

Another quote I found helpful was also from a non-sports source. I was reading *Atlantic Business Magazine* and millionaire

John Risley, a highly regarded business person here on the east coast, wrote an article called "Buyer Beware." It was about making sound investments, and his quote was this: "Real wealth is built or created by entrepreneurs who stay focused on an opportunity and have the skill set necessary to realize it." Bingo! If you substitute the word "success" for "wealth," and "curlers" for "entrepreneurs," you have the magic formula for winning in curling. Funny how these two non-sports people, both wildly successful in their chosen fields, have provided me with some of my best advice.

We all have the energy to be successful; we just have to call it up. We also have a lot of lazy living inside us. Put lazy away, pull out the energy not just for curling, but for everything you do in life, and you'll become a dynamo. Are you ready?

CURLING 101

Just a quick note for the newbies out there... curling is one of those sports that looks much easier than it actually is. If you haven't curled before, don't expect to be able to step on the ice and slide gracefully. Looks can be deceiving. If you're new to the sport, I highly recommend that you attend one of the clinics curling clubs put on for new curlers at the beginning of the year. On top of that, don't be shy about asking any of your fellow curlers for advice—they are only too willing to help out. In the meantime, here's a quick guide to the basics of the game.

Remember that the rock you'll be throwing is a hunk of granite that weighs forty-two pounds! The rock is thrown from the hack, and needs to be released before the first hog line. It needs to cross the second hog line in order to be in play, but it can't go past the backline, which is the line at the back of the house. The house is a series of circles (see diagram 1.1). The outer ring is the twelve-foot, the next circle is called the eight-foot, the smaller circle is the four-foot, and the even-smaller circle is called the button. The area between the house and the hog line is called the free guard zone and when a rock lands there, it must remain in play for the first four rocks of the end (an end is like an inning in baseball). In curling, most club games are now eight ends and so are all the events on the World Curling Tour. But provincial and territorial playdowns and Canadian and world championships are still ten ends, the traditional length of a curling match.

There are four positions on a curling team: the lead throws first, the second throws second, the third, or mate, throws third, and the skip throws last and calls the game. Each player throws two rocks, alternating throws with her opponent. The end is over when all sixteen rocks are thrown. If the score is tied at the end of regulation, you play overtime… except in curling it's called an extra end.

Having the last rock (or hammer) in a given end is considered a huge advantage in this sport—much like being last at bat in baseball. At the club level, a flip of the coin decides who has last rock in the opening end. Then whoever scores in the end concedes the hammer to the other team for the next end. If no rocks remain in the house

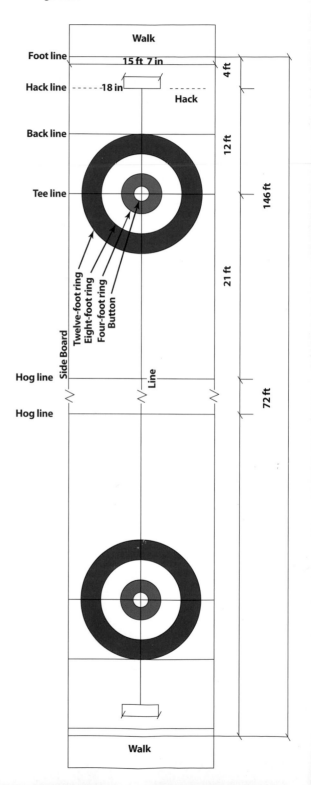

Diagram 1.1
The Curling Sheet

at the conclusion of the end, it is called a "blank end" and no points are scored. After a blank end, the hammer does not change teams. Points are scored by the team whose rocks are closest to the button, and only one team can score in a given end. Any of a team's rocks closer to the button than the other team's rocks count as one point (see diagram 1.2).

So to the beginning curler: Get out and play as often as you can, but don't neglect practice. The bottom line is that in an eight-end game of curling, you'll only throw sixteen rocks, and you won't get much better if that's all you're throwing. Be patient with yourself. Curling is much like golf in that it takes years to understand and perfect so many of the game's nuances, but it's a lifetime sport, so you've got a few years to get it right.

Diagram 1.2

Suppose yellow is sitting four rocks, all in the twelve-foot and the eight-foot. With the last rock in the end (the hammer), red draws to the four-foot. Red would then score one (being closest to the button), yellow wouldn't score any, and yellow would have the hammer in the next end.

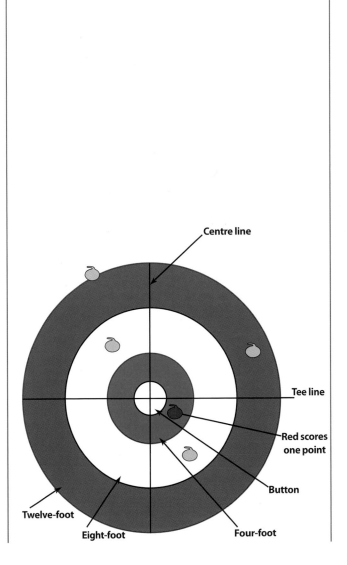

The Gear

Unfortunately for me, when my kids played hockey, they were both goaltenders. The cost of their gear was about three thousand dollars each. Luckily curlers don't have to worry about such expensive equipment. A broom, shoes (usually with a slider that attaches to the shoe for smoother sliding), and a stopwatch are about all a curler needs to get started. Still, by the looks of some curlers' brooms, they're hesitant to spend any money on new equipment.

Arnold Asham is the king of curling equipment in Canada. The red brick Asham slider was his first invention back in 1977, and he's been going strong ever since. He marvels that in curling, unlike other sports, the equipment is often the last thing competitors think about. "I've been in the business for thirty years. Guys will spend a thousand dollars a weekend to go curl. That's their airfare, hotel, entry fee, food, and booze. But people won't spend two or three hundred dollars on the best product," says Arnold.

If you aren't achieving the results you think you should be, take a look at your footwear, the material you slide on. Your footwear is important because it is here where most of your contact with the ice happpens. Does your footwear result in a slide that is too fast or too slow? Is the

COLLEEN'S SECRET

One of the best pieces of advice on strategy was in **The Curling Book** *by Ed Luckowich, Rick Folk, and Paul Gowsell. When planning strategy, they wrote that "skill counts; the best strategy in the world will not win unless your team can make the shots." How true it is. Take baby steps to becoming great. Practice your razzle-dazzle stuff during practice and in league play, but don't bring out the fancy shots in competition unless you have to. Call the shots you know you can make.*

Spend the time (and money) to make sure your sliding surface and broom are up to par.

material too scratched? All of these factors can impact the outcome of a shot. Don't ignore the surface of your back drag leg—it makes contact with the ice, too. "One of the biggest things we are focussing on now is the back foot. The back foot can drag you down, so we're looking at [improving] the toe dip, the plastic cover over the tip of the toe, and the lace cover—anything to cut down on the drag," Arnold explains. The goal is to create a consistent and smooth surface to contact the ice as you slide.

For shoes, I've tried a lot of different sliding surfaces. From the Asham red brick I used in the late 1970s, I graduated to the Pat Ryan (two-time Brier champ) special—stainless steel. I actually loved the stainless, especially on hits, but I couldn't draw with it. Then I tried a sneaker with a Balance Plus slider on it and now I'm back to using the

Asham shoe with double circles on the slider. I think my biggest secret, though, is the duct tape I use on my grip foot to prevent drag. The point I'm emphasizing is to make sure you experiment with your own gear to find the right sliding surface.

COLLEEN'S
SECRET

Kim Kelly always said to us, "Where the mind goes, the behind follows." I think she heard it on Oprah. No matter who said it first, it is very true. You've got to believe. When we were struggling at one particular tournament, Nancy, Kim, and Mary-Anne wrote the letter "B" on their foreheads. The "B" was for believe.

Believe in yourself.

Believe in each other.

Believe in the shot.

Believe you can win.

Believe it is all possible.

As Gerry Peckham told me, "There's no substitute for belief, supported by strong team dynamics."

The other important piece of equipment is your sweeping tool. André Ferland has designed a high-performance broom. These are lightweight, composite broom handles that allow for faster sweeping. "A good sweeper will develop lots of speed, and they are saving energy [by using the lighter broom]. In the long run, at a national [competition], for example, it becomes very important that you aren't wearing down in the middle of the week. On our signature broom there is also a rubberized part that you can't really see, but it allows the sweeper a better grip." Trust me, the broom has come a long way since I started sweeping with my little "Wildcat," an old corn broom with a leather flap along the inside. They don't make these types of brooms anymore, but I sure did love the sound they made on the ice. In my first national tournament, the Canadian Junior Curling Championship, back in the 1970s in Thunder Bay, I was playing second stone. My blisters were so bad by the middle of the week, my hands would bleed. With brooms like that, little wonder I switched to skipping!

I love the newer lightweight, composite push brooms that allow for quick, fast strokes. I still keep a horsehair broom in my broom bag because ice conditions will sometimes make it feel like the cloth foam on the new brooms isn't doing anything. Sometimes you'll also notice that the foam on a composite broom feels wet by the fifth end; that's when I prefer to go with hair.

Another essential piece of curling equipment today is the stopwatch. I'll never forget curling in my first world championship in 1982 in Geneva, Switzerland. I'd get ready to throw my last rock and ask my sisters, Barb and Monica, what the ice was like. They would say things like, "it's heavy," or "it's really keen," or my favourite, "it's like normal ice back home on a good day." It was all fairly vague, subjective information. But that's how ice was judged back then. In Switzerland that year, the ice was a disaster. It must have been sloped—it was lightning fast one way and take-out weight for draw weight the other way. Needless to say, when it came to throwing draw weight we were just guessing, and our results were less than impressive. I don't think I've ever played on worse ice, but that was pretty much par for the course back in the eighties at the international level—thankfully things have changed a lot since then.

The stopwatch would have been a big help to us at those worlds in Geneva, and it's been a huge innovation—most curlers today time every shot during a match. With split times—timing from the backline to the first hog line—sweepers get an early idea of where the rock should land, and this makes for better shot-making. But don't be a slave to the stopwatch. Don Bartlett, one of the best leads to ever play the game, relied on his uncanny ability to eyeball draw weight when he was sweeping. And he was rarely wrong, always sweeping Kevin Martin's rocks perfectly to the button. The times between the two hog lines can also be useful, and often more reliable, since the split time taken

COLLEEN'S
SECRET

While corn brooms are dead, you can still practise your sweeping on the kitchen floor with your push broom. Simulate a game situation, sweeping hard for twenty-five seconds, rest for a minute. Do another twenty-five seconds, rest for a minute. This is an awesome drill, but really quite tough. Try for sixty reps, the same amount of time a front end would sweep in a game if they were sweeping all draws.

between backline and hog line can vary so much from shooter to shooter.

Ferland, while recognizing what a great tool the watch is, also cautions against overusing it. "The advantage with time is you can communicate with the skip right from the beginning. But be careful, because there is often a difference between curler to curler with split times, so you have to know your team really well. If all the curlers have the same technique, they'll have the same time. But some curlers have a fast slide and pull back at release; others slow down faster and once in a while curlers will add weight on release and then your timing won't be right. So the sweepers have to recognize that and not totally rely on the stopwatch." Wise words. But I still wish we had been using one in Switzerland back in 1982.

The Ice

Having good gear is important but it's not worth much if the ice you're playing on isn't any good. I remember having this discussion with Pal Trulsen from Norway, the Olympic gold medalist, in 2002. We were talking about how there are two kinds of curling… club curling and arena curling. For those of us like Pal and I who have been lucky to play in plenty of arena events, we have been spoiled. Arena ice has usually been babied, coddled, and groomed to perfection. In a curling club, not so much.

Mark Sharek, the icemaker for the World Curling Tour, is known for producing perfect ice and rock conditions, and agrees that curlers are often surprised by the difference between club ice and arena ice:

> In a curling club the ice is almost always a little straighter and a little heavier. One of the biggest variables [in an arena] is the crowd because of the heat load. Also, how much sweeping is done in your game can be a factor in pebble breakdown. Plus what time of day you're curling at has an impact. If you're curling on a morning draw, the building is colder, and things are crisper. Rocks in the morning are colder—about thirty-four degrees Fahrenheit; in the afternoon the rocks could be up to thirty-five, and these warmer rocks will be straighter. Also, if the pebble breaks down in the later ends it usually makes rocks go a little straighter.

Understanding the science of icemaking can help your game enormously. Watching for the subtle changes that happen to the ice you're playing on is important. Often we skips are guilty of playing one side of the sheet exclusively for the first two ends. Then we'll finally throw a draw down the other side of the sheet in the third end, only to have the draw come up six feet short. Mark explained that curlers will often come off the ice and complain one side is heavier than the other. "But what they forget is that they ignored one side of the sheet for two ends. That's a half hour with no rocks going down it, so of course it might be a little heavier because it just sat there." Again, there are a lot of variables in this game, but that slippery surface you stand on is really the most crucial.

BUT NOT JUST ANY OLD PRACTICE WILL DO!

By my rough calculations, I've thrown about 225,000 practice rocks. This doesn't take into account the rocks I throw in games… simply practice. There have been many, many practices where I've just mindlessly thrown rocks, and this is fine. That mindless throwing when you're on automatic pilot can serve you well in pressure games when your delivery has to be so dialled in that you could do it in your sleep.

But on top of mindless practice, you also need solid team practices with specific goals. My team had great practices scheduled three times a week (and on the days we were not practising, we were expected to practise on our own). We spent the first end throwing the rocks up and warming up our slide and the ice. Then we went to work. From the second end on, we threw in order of position with full sweeping and stopwatches. I had the easy part—I just held the broom. While a lot of coaches want to call the shots and ice, I think it's more beneficial for the skip to do this in order to know his or her teammates' tendencies. In the second end, we did a hit drill, throwing two in-turn and out-turn hits each. Nancy would start with her four, then Mary-Anne, then Kim, and lastly, I would throw mine. If someone missed a shot that everyone else made, the thrower would try to figure out why. Did I underthrow it? Did I turn it in? Did I throw it in or out? Learn to critique your own delivery and release. Any time you miss, make sure you ask yourself why. (Believe me, it's not always that the skip has the broom in the wrong place.)

In the third end, when we've hopefully "keened" the ice up a bit (keen ice is fast ice), we start throwing draws. Again, each team member throws identical shots to reveal any differences between teammates. Full sweeping is on, and we throw two in-turns and two out-turns. Paul Savage, who won a Brier and a world title playing for Ed Werenich, gave me a great tip years ago about practising draw weight. He said to throw two exact out-turn draws using the same broom while trying to make your weight identical. Pay attention to your leg

drive and also check for the curl of the rocks—this is a great way to match rocks, too. Just keep throwing two rocks up and two rocks back. When you're doing this drill, make sure someone is calling out exactly what the weight is. If you're by yourself, follow the rocks up the ice and call out loud exactly what kind of weight you think you threw.

In the fourth end, we move onto my personal favourite—my team calls it progressives (and if the terminology that follows is over your head, don't despair—there's a handy curling glossary at the end of this book). This time we each throw five rocks in a row. It starts with a centre guard already in place. Nancy's first shot is simple—a come-around to the eight-foot. The second shot is backline weight, tapping the first rock out. The third shot is hack weight, tapping the second rock out. The fourth is a hit and roll behind the centre guard, and the fifth shot is peeling out the shot behind the guard. This incorporates a variety of shot weights and is useful because it showed us all how throwing the wrong weight impacted the outcome of the shot. If you throw hack weight on a shot where the broom is in place for backline, you miss it badly. So this drill really encouraged us not to be cavalier about our weight choices during a game. If backline was called for, we threw backline. By having the broom in the same spot for all five shots, we could clearly see people's tendencies on certain turns and

COLLEEN'S
SECRET

Enjoy practice! Work hard and get a lot out of your practices, but have fun. We always laughed and gabbed our way through our practices. If you're going to make it too much like work you'll never last. So work hard, but enjoy the process.

then work to correct them. In the fifth end we'd make the same throws as the fourth end, except we'd play the other turn into the middle or throw to the wings. So if we threw all in-turns in the previous end, we'd do all out-turns in the next end. The sixth end was a bit of everything. We'd either work on a shot that had been giving us trouble, or practice run backs, or have an end of straight peeling. Individual practices were a chance to be honest with ourselves about what we were struggling with, especially any persistent throwing or delivery problems.

If I find myself with what I think is a delivery problem, I have a favourite drill that usually helps correct whatever flaw I have. Try it sometime when you're having a tough time with your delivery. Grab a plastic beer cup from the club's bar, put it at the first hog line, and just slide to it. Are you sliding consistently wide or tight? Play with your slide. If you shift your knees two millimetres to the right or left in the hack does this impact your slide? If you move your slide foot a little bit does this change the slide? Keep adjusting until you find a consistent slide and know you're "in the zone."

I spoke to former Brier champ, Olympian, and World Curling Tour champion Kevin Martin recently about his seemingly flawless technique, and he revealed his own method for solving a delivery problem. Anytime he has a throwing problem, he says "it's never release, it's always line of delivery." When it goes wacky, he calls his coach, Jules Owchar, who he says "has an amazing eye for the mechanics; he's just so good at seeing what's wrong." Clearly, Jules is a genius because he's been with Kevin since juniors and Kevin's longevity and success are second to none.

What Jules does for Kevin is line up rocks along the path of the delivery. "If the problem is early in my slide, we put the rocks closer to the backline. I just keep throwing until I get the line right." The other thing Kevin does is practise a lot, especially in the days leading up to a big event. "I'll throw a lot, maybe not as many as the old days, but I'll throw a lot of draws and taps, always with sweeping because you've got to make it as real as possible. So if I'm by myself, I'll jump up and sweep my own rocks." Having practised alongside another former Brier champ, Mark Dacey, at our home club, the

COLLEEN'S SECRET

I interviewed Glenn Howard the morning after he won the 2007 Brier in Hamilton. He said the secret to his and brother Russ's success (Russ, of course, won Olympic gold with Brad Gushue in 2006) lay with their father. "Dad was an advocate of teaching proper technique and the proper delivery. Russ and I have similar deliveries, and we were always taught that if you have proper technique it will never let you down in any pressure situation." Pressure is something the Howard boys seem to thrive on. When it comes to rock throwing, their technique is as close to perfection as you can get. Clearly dear old dad taught them well.

Mayflower Curling Club, I know that this is also a trademark of Mark's. His practices are always focussed—he often throws alone, and, like Martin, he sweeps every single rock. (Little wonder he ended Nova Scotia's long drought at the Brier with his win over Randy Ferbey in 2004.)

So when you're on the ice practising, focus on specific goals and demand results from yourself and your team. It's the only way you'll see improvement in your game: if you keep doing the same old thing, you'll keep getting the same outcome. Because the slide is such an important technique to practice (and practice and practice), it is the subject of the next chapter.

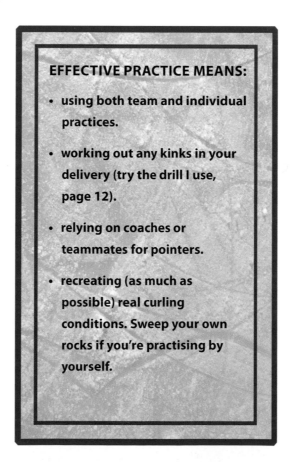

EFFECTIVE PRACTICE MEANS:

- using both team and individual practices.

- working out any kinks in your delivery (try the drill I use, page 12).

- relying on coaches or teammates for pointers.

- recreating (as much as possible) real curling conditions. Sweep your own rocks if you're practising by yourself.

MASTERING THE PERFECT SLIDE

One of the books I devoured when I was a kid was *Ken Watson on Curling*. Watson was a three-time Brier winner way back in the 1930s and 1940s. While much of the book is irrelevant now, he was absolutely correct when he wrote, "The importance of mastering the mechanics of a well-balanced swing or delivery in curling cannot be over-emphasized." Master your slide, make it perfect for you, and you will succeed. All of the top teams have this secret down. Teams that are in the also-ran department don't pay enough attention to the need for a great slide. But you can only achieve a good slide through practice and self-

Balance and a smooth release are two of the keys to perfecting your sliding technique.

criticism. It certainly helps to have a trusted coach to work with during some of your practices.

My team has been lucky enough to work with some great curling teachers. Scott Taylor from Balance Plus was able to show us, through the magic of videotape and lasers, where we had a few hiccups in our mechanics. Gerry Peckham also spent many hours with us working on mechanics. And the great Rick Folk, a two-time Brier and world champion, also spent several seasons advising and tweaking our form. The secret to winning and improving is to keep an open mind and ear. Don't ever believe, just because your slide looks pretty, that it's good enough. In my twenty trips to the national women's championships, everyone had a reasonable-looking slide, yet they still missed a lot of shots. Why? All style, no substance. They slid nicely, but their release was ugly. They slid nicely, but one shoulder dipped two inches below the other. They slid nicely, but always tight. Like Ken Watson said, the

importance of mastering the slide cannot be overemphasized.

One other brilliant thing the legendary Ken Watson wrote decades ago that is still considered gospel is this: "no two curlers deliver a stone alike." This still rings true today. A lot of coaches that I've watched seem to want everyone to throw exactly the same way. You can throw on your toe like Jeff Stoughton, you can throw with your toe turned way in like Don Walchuck, or be perfectly classic like Glenn Howard—all of these different deliveries work perfectly well.

I interviewed the great Randy Ferbey, skip of the fabulous Ferbey Four (Ferbey, of course, has won six Canadian championships and an amazing four world curling championships). He tucks, still lifts the rock, and throws with the broom propped over his shoulder—as he said to me, his delivery is "ugly." But does anyone make prettier shots? "Am I saying it's the best way to throw? No," Ferbey says. "Is it the worst? No, it's not. I can throw more weight than ninety percent of the flat-footers. If I was starting curling today, would I have an ugly slide like mine or a pretty slide like they teach? I'd probably choose the pretty slide. But my slide really works for me and you've got to find the delivery that works for you. There are all kinds of golf swings out there; the same is true for the curling delivery. Do what works for you." Those are wise words from one of the best curlers in the game. Why is his delivery so reliable? "My slide gives me stability. From my shoulders to my chest, I'm stable and perfectly square. So I may not slide perfectly all the time, but I'm square to the broom."

"I guess my experience would tell me there's no such thing as a perfect delivery," agrees Gerry Peckham, director of high performance for the Canadian Curling Association. "We have seen so many elite players get the job done differently. So there's more than one way to seek performance

Randy Ferbey: "There are all kinds of golf swings out there; the same is true for the curling delivery. Do what works for you."

perfection without taking a cookie-cutter approach."

As Watson says, no one throws the same way, and often beauty is in the eye of the beholder. But there are a few basic ingredients that make a slide smooth: balance, sliding on line, and proper grip and release.

Balance is one of the most important elements of a good slide—a little wobble is enough to make you lose focus as you take that split second to recover. As Gerry Peckham explains: "Basically you need one hundred percent balance, one hundred percent of the time. There's no margin for error in balance because it affects everything else. Balance is simply the predominant element. The line of delivery would be next and then the release is third—making [the rock] go where you need it to go."

And if your release is not pure, all the pretty sliding in the world is for naught. Of course, sliding on line is also important. If you're a little off line at the start of your delivery, by the time the stone reaches the hog line, you'll often find the shot misses by a good margin.

Another book I devoured as a kid was Ernie Richardson's *Curling Techniques and Strategy*, and again, while certain chapters are now totally obsolete, the section on proper grip is still useful. Richardson writes, "The fingers all play different roles during the delivery. The thumb gives you the feel of the

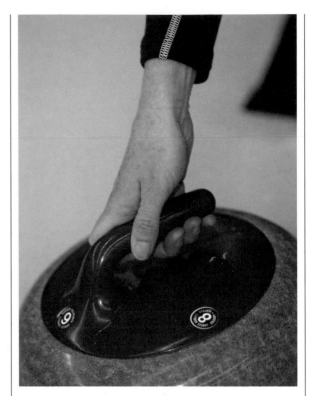

Don't make the mistake of holding the rock too tightly. Your fourth and fifth fingers should be applying very little pressure.

rock and along with the little fingers it permits you to apply the particular turn you want for the shot. The index finger provides most of the pressure throughout the delivery with help from the middle finger. The fourth finger goes along mostly for the ride. The little finger applies practically no pressure but helps guide the rock during delivery." Many juniors I see at my club or during clinics have a death-grip hold on their rock. I don't know how, when it comes time for the release, they can possibly pry it out of their hands. Your grip affects the release, which affects the shot, so lighten up a little; don't kill the poor little handle.

Even with good balance, a clean slide, and a proper grip, from time to time you may lose your rhythm and your delivery may go haywire. I recommend using individual practice for working on your mechanics. Take your coach, a teammate, or ask someone in your club who's knowledgeable for a little help.

I recommend doing this during individual practice time because to work out kinks takes a lot of repetition, and it is best not to waste your precious team practice time. Another drill I use to work on mechanics again uses beer cups. Take two beer cups, put them at the hog line with just enough room

COLLEEN'S SECRET

Mark Nichols, Olympic gold medalist, gave me this tip when we were speaking at a coaching symposium. In order to work on your big-weight shots, shots Mark excels at, he suggests this: "Have the icemaker put two or three pebbles on the ice for practice and throw away. I grew up on really heavy ice at the Carol Curling Club in Labrador, so I was able to throw big weight. It's all leg drive; my legs are my strongest muscles. But it does take a lot of practice to throw big weight well. I kind of jump with my sliding foot for more power." The big-weight shot is a weapon all the great men's teams have. If you want to get better at throwing big-weight shots, ask your icemaker to make conditions really heavy for you by adding more pebble.

for your slide to squeeze through. Then put a third cup between the two but position it back about five feet from the hog line. Now slide with a rock at that third cup, trying not to disturb the two cups at the hog line. If you're always hitting the outside cup, you're sliding a bit wide, so simply adjust your

position in the hack a few millimetres to the right. If you're always hitting the inside cup, adjust the other way.

My second drill is to remove the cups and put a rock eight feet beyond the first hog line. Your goal is to keep hitting it on the nose (or a little on the high side). If you're

hitting it on the high side and rolling over to the other sheet, you're sliding too wide, so keep doing this until you're nailing it consistently on the nose. Keep moving the target around, and throw all sixteen rocks like this. Then, in the next end and on your way back, do the same drill, but this time set the rocks in the house. You should see a big improvement.

Videotaping is another useful tool in finding problems in your delivery. Videotape yourself when you're throwing perfectly, and keep it on file. When you're in one of those inevitable slumps, videotape yourself again and compare it to the tape of your perfect delivery. Often you'll quickly see the problem. For me, it's usually that I'm getting too low, too quickly in my delivery. It might be a difference of just a few centimetres, but it's enough to throw off my rhythm.

My fourth suggestion is a draw drill I learned from Paul Savage that I like to do when I'm in a draw funk. Have a practice where all you're doing is throwing two draws up and two draws back the other way, over and over and over again. Keep doing the drill until you nail above the tee line weight six times. One great tip Gerry Peckham gave me was to stop aiming for the button when I'm practising by myself, since it doesn't factor in the impact sweepers can make, so aim for the twelve-foot or the eight-foot. As long as

COLLEEN'S
SECRET

For better balance, slide without your broom, and try throwing a few rocks. Then go back to delivering with your broom; you'll be surprised how balanced and easy it seems. Another great balance finder is to throw with your eyes closed. Do this three or four times either with or without a rock. Try it with your broom and without it. You'll be surprised how easy your delivery seems when you throw with your eyes open.

I can throw top-twelve weight consistently in practice, I know I'm set. I'm also good at timing my own rocks when I practise; it is a great idea to guess what you threw and then confirm it with your clock. In the beginning I was always way off. I would think I threw a 14.5 seconds between the hogs, but the clock consistently showed 13.9 (draw weight is typically 14.3 to 14.5 on arena ice). I eventually got very good at this game and it helped my draw weight become more consistent. And the bottom line is, if you can't draw, you can't win.

The ingredients to a smooth slide: balance, sliding on line, and proper grip and release.

WORKING AS A TEAM

Curling is a unique sport in the sense that the delivery of each shot is very much an individual act. But once the rock leaves your hands, it takes the whole team to make the shot, from the sweepers to the teammates calling the line. Team work is essential; each and every team member must be working as one. This isn't always as easy as it sounds, but working together as a team is certainly easier with good team chemistry.

Chemistry is one of the hardest things to quantify, but it's essential on a winning team. Sure, some teams can win without chemistry, but they don't last and the season usually winds up being torture. It's hard to know how to achieve great chemistry, but all teams know when they've got it, and they know when they don't. When Mary-Anne Arsenault joined our team in 1999, our team clicked and we had instant chemistry. Not only could she shoot the lights out, but she had a quiet yet strong presence on the team. When she spoke it was usually because she had something important to say. She was our missing link. Even though Kim, Nancy, and I had been together for a while, without Mary-Anne we had no mojo, we were just another team chasing a dream.

From left: Colleen Jones, Kim Kelly, Mary-Anne Arsenault, and Nancy Delahunt.
The foursome captured five Canadian women's curling championships
between 1999 and 2004.

Over the years, I had juggled lineups and tried new people, but there was always something missing. It was simple when I won the Canadian championship for the first time in 1982 with my two sisters, Monica and Barb, and my friend, Kay Zinck. We were all university students with no commitments or worries. But as you get older and try to find the balance between curling, family, and work, getting the right personnel becomes more complicated. Everyone might be committed and on board during the off-season, but when push comes to shove, you may find some people don't have the real commitment it takes to win. The time bonspielling, practising, and preparing is not for everyone. When you're putting together a team, be sure to consider how much time each person can commit to competing and practising and make sure the various personalities fit well together. If the personalities don't fit, there's no magic wand you can wave to make it work. You simply have to juggle the lineup or the personnel until you find a combination that works.

Mark Nichols agrees. "Chemistry is very important, more important than having the four best shooters," he says. "You need people who accept their position on the team. Someone has to be a cheerleader, maybe someone's more serious. You really need the right mix of individuals."

Chemistry is magic when you find it, though. "If you could figure out why chemistry works and how, you'd make a million dollars," Randy Ferbey says. "But it's everything to a winning team. Comparing our team, we've been together for eight years now—the only reason other teams don't stick together is they stop getting along."

So when putting together a team, you don't necessarily need the top four throwers, but you do need four people who will support, believe, and commit to the long journey it takes to become a champion. But those are just the people on the ice during the game. On our winning teams, our two fifths, Laine Peters and Mary Sue Radford, were absolutely instrumental to our success. They scouted, they matched rocks, they arranged schedules—they both played more of a coaching role. They always had a profound observation after every game and pearls of wisdom before them.

Of course, it also helps to have teammates who understand their roles and know what they need to do to help the team excel. When we won our first Canadian championship in 1999, we were decent enough players. By the time we won our fifth Canadian championship, Nancy, Mary-Anne, and Kim really owned their positions. They were perennial all-stars, and Kim, who played every position for me in our fifteen years together, was a Canadian all-star at

Nancy Delahunt

lead, second, and third—I'm sure that's a record! In their own words, here is how each member of our team contributed to team success.

The Lead

by Nancy Delahunt

Every position on a curling team has its importance, but all too often teams make the mistake of leaving a weak player at the lead position, possibly because talented, competitive curlers are often not motivated to play this position. I truly loved my position and found endless ways to improve my own play and contribute to other aspects of the team.

The easiest advice I can give is to make your shots and outplay the opposition. I was never one to look at stats, but I knew by the end of a game whether I had held up my end of the bargain. Components of putting my best game together included:

1) Smart individual practices. My favourite drill was to set up a centre guard and targets that represented the broom. I would throw four draws at a time: an in-turn and an out-turn around the centre guard (positioned in front of the tee), then draws

to each wing. I would clear these, and then repeat. As the year progressed, I would score "four out of four" more frequently. During individual practising, I would also work on my trouble spot of the week. There was always something to work on.

2) Minimizing that cardinal sin. Long centre guards are unforgivable, unless it's the final end of the game without hammer. In a close match when I'm throwing a centre

COLLEEN'S SECRET

One of my favourite motivational books is Phil Jackson's Sacred Hoops. In it he writes, "The team with the greatest dedication, desire, and single-minded effort ends up winning." This is so true, especially the need for single-minded effort. I was lucky to find Nancy, Kim, and Mary-Anne, three other women with the same goals and commitment level. We all got along and we all totally believed in each other. That belief took us a long way.

guard without hammer (whether it's the first rock of the end, or guarding a rock in the four-foot), I would much rather be in the house than long. Corner guards can generally be a bit longer, depending on ice conditions.

3) Doing the simple things well. Colleen would often reflect that it was the simple shot that turned an end around—the hit and roll out, for example. As a lead, when hitting a rock in the wings with a centre guard in place (with hammer), you must stick.

4) Having a clear plan to deal with pressure. Try to find something to fill your mind, something that you get to choose—a song, a thought, a specific delivery trigger, or some sort of mantra. Without a plan, the pressure of the moment will occupy your mind, and it could be ugly.

5) Looking forward to that "key" shot. As a lead, I didn't get many of the fancy shots, but I licked my lips when they came my way. Many players hope for the easy shot, but the "fancy" shot was what I most wanted.

Mary-Anne Arsenault

6) Committing to each and every shot—whether you like the call or not.

On our team, I also held the broom for Colleen's shots, and this job came with its own set of responsibilities. Generally I believe that up to eighty percent of a team's success in a game relates to the confidence level of the skip. I felt that part of my responsibility was to positively affect our skip's level of play, which inevitably was relative to her level of confidence. Feedback is great; positive feedback is even better.

I believe that skips are typically able to decipher their own mistakes or miscues. There is rarely a need to recall all errors and possible causes.

The Second

by Mary-Anne Asenault

The role of a second varies from team to team. The qualities found in a great second on any team include, firstly, being a consistent shot-maker. Setting up play for the back end (the third and skip) is essential

Kim Kelly

to a team's success. My job was to make the key hit and roll or perfect draw behind a guard, shots crucial for multiple-point ends. Secondly, a good second needs to be an effective sweeper. That entails judging weight appropriately as well as the actual task of moving the brush. Thirdly, and arguably most importantly, a second needs to be a team player. Being able to put the team's needs first and letting any little issues slide is crucial. A second may assume many other roles, such as team organizer or cheerleader, depending on the team's dynamic. My role on the team was one of quiet confidence and support. If asked for input, I gave it. If not asked, I rarely offered unsolicited advice.

The Third

by Kim Kelly

The obvious advice I can give for how to become the best third you can be would be to say that you must make all your shots, but how do you do that? First, and most importantly, you must decide whether you have the desire and passion to put yourself out there, take the time necessary to be the best, and truly make curling a priority. I see improvements to your game falling into three main categories: technical skill, physical fitness, and mental preparedness.

Technical skill

The best way to improve and maintain optimal technical ability is to practise, but you must practise with purpose. Set goals for your practices, figure out how to achieve those goals and then set about meeting them. At practice, you must be engaged. Going through the motions won't work.

How often you should practice depends on your curling goals. You need enough to be physically prepared (but not so much your body always aches), enough for good performance (but not so much that you burn out), and just enough to allow yourself time for other commitments.

Physical fitness

Physical fitness is essential for optimizing performance. Again, set goals and develop a plan to achieve them. It really is worth getting input from a fitness professional, but like anything in life, you have to "just do it." How many times do people set goals, develop a plan, and then stop? This is especially true for fitness training. The next time you find yourself rationalizing why you deserve to skip your workout today, remember: no pain, no gain. It is a very powerful thing to arrive at a competition knowing you have done all you can do to prepare.

Eat and sleep well. This seems obvious but is so important, especially during long competitions. Finally, look after those aches and pains with regular massage, a chiropractor, or physiotherapy—whatever works.

Mental preparedness

Learning a new mental skill is just like learning a physical one. It takes practice. You cannot change a behaviour by simply stating, "I am not going to do that anymore." Like fitness training, consult a specialist for help. A good sports psychologist is priceless.

Believe you can do it. A lot of this confidence comes from knowing you did all you could to be ready to compete.

Be in the moment. This is easy to say but takes work to really do it. This is a mental skill that takes a lot of practice, especially for women. You can't be somewhere else worrying about other aspects of your life when you're trying to curl at a competitive level. You need a good support system—your family, friends, and employer all need to be on board with your goals.

Believe in your teammates and remember you are one unit. The team as a whole should be stronger than the sum of its parts. So you have to accept and bless each individual for all their strengths and weaknesses. Respect is essential.

Have a single-minded focus. Remember you are not playing for yourself alone; you are part of a team. Do not take things personally, but honestly recognize your strengths and weaknesses. You will get the most out of what you have to work with if

you maximize your strengths. There is no time for pride or jealousy. My favourite quotes on this topic: "It is amazing what you can accomplish if you do not care who gets the credit," from Harry Truman; "Nobody can make you feel inferior without your permission," from Eleanor Roosevelt.

Lastly, but most importantly, remember to enjoy the experience and have fun. Make the effort to inject fun into the hard work.

The Skip

I echo all the points Nancy, Mary-Anne, and Kim make. Shot-making, fitness, and mental toughness are all crucial, and to be a great skip, they are even more necessary. As skip, you want to make that last shot. You're dying to have the rock in your hand with the game on the line, and you know you can execute. If you don't believe this totally, you should look at playing another position.

I always saw my role on the team from a throwing perspective as this: close the deal. My teammates have set me up, and it's my job to finish it off. Like a goalie who lets in a soft goal and causes a team's confidence and momentum to fizzle, if, as a skip, you miss a gimme draw or roll out when you're supposed to hit it on the nose, you've let down your team.

You're forgiven if you miss the run back or if you jam on the double, but never miss the easy shots. There will be games with the team in a hopeless situation and you have to throw a Hail Mary in order to score—sometimes these situations are totally unavoidable and sometimes you skipped your way into the jam you're looking at. After the game, review all of your shots, think of the turning points in each end, and decide what calls were just plain stupid and what calls were great but suffered from poor execution.

It is easy to be the skip when things are going really well and everyone's making their shots. But nobody curls one hundred percent. There will be misses, and some will be ugly. This is when skipping becomes

Colleen Jones

interesting. When execution fails, the original game plan is thrown out the window and you need to improvise. As skip, it's my job to quickly weigh the best option for the particular thrower, based on the ice conditions, what the score is, and where we are in the end.

For a skip, having that sixth sense about whether to play conservatively or go for

A good skip listens to teammates and encourages their input.

broke is crucial, and games are won and lost on what skips call "gut instinct." But again, use some common sense—the goal of the game you're playing is not to come in second, so balance defense with offense and bravado with caution.

The most important trait for a skip is the ability to let go. It is easy to carry over the effects of one bad end to the next, or one bad shot to the next, but if you can't put negative events out of your mind, you are doomed. This, of course, is one of the toughest things in the game: the distinction between what has already happened, what you cannot control, and what is happening now. This only comes with practice, unfortunately. One day you just realize that holding onto the past doesn't serve any purpose.

The other thing a skip has to do well is listen. While the skip calls the shots and reads the ice, the other three people on the team are bright, capable players who will often see things developing in the game, in the ice, or in the rocks that you might be missing. So let them know you want to hear from them and be open to them. My team was also helpful in telling me if they noticed a throwing problem with one of our players, since we were so accustomed to how we all threw. This input made reading and calling the ice more effective. As sweepers they would have a bird's-eye view of the release and quietly let me know if they noticed a throwing flaw that might affect the shot. It was valuable information for reading the ice.

Finally, a skip has to remain positive. While your first reaction might be negative, if someone throws a long guard, try to see the possibilities and remain positive with what has transpired. If, as skip, you are not positive and confident, your teammates will sense it in a hurry and one bad shot can lead to another.

THE CURLING WORKOUT

When I covered the Canadian Open golf tournament in Ancaster in 2006, I was able to see the workout trailers for the golfers. In an effort to compete with Tiger Woods, whose workout regime is renowned, golfers have jumped on the fitness bandwagon. Curling is a lot like golf—sure, you can play without being the fittest person on the block, but you might wind up wondering how much better you could be. At the Brier or Tournament of Hearts, there are a number of players with knee or back problems—could a different workout regime prevent those injuries? If you lose toward the end of the round robin or playoffs, was it because, frankly, you were worn out? If you had been fitter, would the results have been any different?

What role fitness plays in the winning equation is really hard to say, but I would argue that it is often the missing ingredient. My team was lucky to be able to work with two great trainers, Leo Thornley and Darren Steeves. They are both experts who work with athletes at the Canadian Sport Centre. While they gave us a workout for the entire body, I took what worked for me and fit it into the time I had. They gave me an hour-

and-a-half program that I whittled down to about half an hour, because, let's face it, when you have a career, children to raise, dinner to cook, and bonspiels to win, there are only so many hours in a day. Yet, I totally believe fitness is crucial to winning. The gist of what the centre came up with after looking at my curling delivery was that I needed to maintain and improve flexibility and I needed strong legs to reduce wobbling out of the hack, for more accurate shot-making.

Strong quads and hamstrings also help protect your knees, and, knock on wood, my knees have never once complained or ached. So, with the usual warning that you should consult your doctor before embarking on a fitness program (I also recommend that you use a personal trainer for a few sessions to make sure your form is sound), here is my "Half-hour to Great Curling Workout." I never do cardio at the gym, by the way. I ride my bike to work, I play tennis, or I walk the dog—something fun that I really

don't consider "working out." I refuse to run (except in tennis), for fear the constant pounding on pavement could hurt my knees. In curling, the health of your knees is everything. Many a curler's career has been ruined by bad knees, so make sure you're very careful about how you treat them.

Obviously use the weights that work for you. I choose to do two sets of fifteen

COLLEEN'S SECRET

When I interviewed Randy Ferbey he said the best advice he ever got for his delivery came from his trusted front end buddy, Dennis Sutton, back around 1980 when curlers were just starting to use deliveries with no backswing. Randy and Dennis were playing front end for the Friendly Giant— Brier champion Hec Gervais. "Dennis told me to never change that little hitch in my backswing. It was great advice. Why does the hitch work? I don't know. Maybe it's a timing thing like a baseball player and his swing. I don't know why it works, but it works and you don't change what works."

reps instead of the prescribed three, simply because I have more important things to do! I rest for about forty-five seconds between sets. If you're a newbie to the stability ball or the bosu, work on your balance on those before incorporating weights. I've chosen the portion of the workout that I continue through the curling season and it's one that you can do at home. I recommend investing in a few hand weights, a stability ball, and a bosu. The convenience of being able to workout at home is a huge time saver.

The Warm-Up

I love this exercise because it improves your leg strength and you can really feel your ankles, an underrated and very important part of a strong curling delivery, working for balance. Turn the bosu upside down and stand on the flat side. Holding five-pound weights, squat down while bringing your arms straight in front of you, stopping your hand movement at eye level (top and bottom photos). Repeat fifteen times and do two sets.

Remember to keep your back straight and don't let your knees go over your toes. Keep your neck and shoulders relaxed while pulling your arms straight up to eye level. Keep your core strong and remember to breathe.

If you're just beginning, try it without the weights to start. If it's your first time on the bosu, you might want to practice by a wall first.

Still Warming Up

This is my ultimate curling delivery strengthener. Arrange the step to your level of comfort (I like to use two blocks under it). You're going to lunge and curl (I use ten-pound weights) at the same time (top and middle photos).

Do a practice lunge to make sure you're coming down at a ninety-degree angle and that your knee doesn't come over your toes (although I certainly know that in the curling delivery, your knee is coming over your toes all the time).

Do fifteen lunges on the left side, doing curls with both arms on the way down. Take a little break, then do the right side.

Then we flip it. Put your right toe down on the step, lunge with your left leg, and curl your arms at the same time (bottom photo, previous page). Do fifteen lunges on each side.

Just for Good Measure—Squats with the Ball

I probably don't need to do this exercise because the first two have me covered, but I do one more anyway.

With the stability ball between your back and the wall (top photo), roll down the wall and get into the chair position (with the ball still at your back). Hold at the bottom for a count of two. I do two sets of fifteen.

Stability Ball Strength

This exercise also focusses on leg and core strength, but without weights. Lie on your back, and put your heels on the stability ball (middle photo).

Keep your shoulders and head on the mat, and lift your butt. Now curl the ball in toward you, using slow, controlled movements (bottom photo, opposite page). Keep your core strong, and don't let your butt sag to the floor. Do two sets of fifteen.

Now we'll do the opposite. Put your stomach on the ball. Your hands prop you up and should be under your shoulders. Now roll the ball down your body to your toes, so that the front of your toes are on the ball (top photo). Hold this position for a bit to get your balance. Keep your core strong by engaging the abdominal muscles. Now roll the ball into your chest. Do two sets of fifteen. I love this exercise—I feel like it's working every muscle in my body.

Now, let's incorporate some weights. With your shoulders and upper back on the stability ball and feet planted on the floor (middle photo), do fifteen bicep builders slowly. Three seconds up, three seconds down. Surely this has got to help a little for sweeping power. Do two sets of fifteen.

And just because you're here, throw in some tricep work (bottom photo, previous page). From the same position as the bicep builder, simply bring your hands over your head and lift up and down slowly. Really isolate your tricep and don't let your hands come too far forward on the upswing. The stability ball is wonderful because while you may be primarily working your triceps, obviously your legs are still engaged, and your core has to stay strong to provide the stability. You get a lot of bang for your buck with the stability ball.

For Flexibility

The sweaty part of the workout is over, but because I'm not a flexible person, the hard part is about to begin. I have taken a lot of yoga classes and incorporate yoga into my half-hour workout, using the yoga stretches that best fit for curlers (although one could argue that just about all yoga stretches help for curlers). Yoga is gentle, so go easy and do what your body allows in the stretch. I worked with Robert Webber at the Yoga Loft and consulted with him about what stretches I should incorporate for curling strength. He recommended that I focus on my hip flexor muscles and balance-strengthening poses. These poses are best done in bare feet, but I'm often at a curling club doing these in my curling shoes before a game. These exercises have really helped my balance out of the hack, and keep me curling ready during the off-season. I also find it helps with my overall core strength, which helps prevent any back issues.

(top photo). Close your eyes to improve your balance. Breathe. Do this for five deep breaths, visualizing drawing to the button for the win. Repeat and do your other side for five breaths.

From here we move to the curler's lunge with a twist. Start with the same lunge pose as the previous exercise. Your left knee is at a ninety-degree angle over your left foot. Your right knee is lifted off the mat. Plant your right hand by your foot. Lift your left arm into the air, slowly twisting your body around to look up at your left hand (bottom photo). Breathe for five deep breaths. Visualize making a perfect hit and roll. Then switch legs and stretch the other side.

The Curler's Lunge

Assume a "lunging" position, with one leg extended straight behind you and the other at an angle in front of you. Your front foot should be flat on the floor. Instead of your thigh and lower leg making a forty-five degree angle (like they would in a proper curling delivery), change it to a healthier ninety degrees with your left knee directly over your left foot. Now bring your back right knee off the mat. Hold steady and breathe. Lift your hands off the floor when and if you feel strong enough, eventually bringing them straight over your head

The Tree Pose

This exercise is in my top three for overall strength and stretch for the whole body. Once again, like when working on the bosu, I find this really helps my ankle strength, which in turn keeps me strong driving out of the hack. If you're just starting out, you can do this exercise against a wall.

Ground your right foot, solidly on the floor. Slowly lift your left foot and place it where it feels good for you, either on the calf or the thigh. As your balance improves, put your hands on your hips and eventually over your head (top photo). Hold for five deep breaths. Visualize yourself making that run back for the win. Then open the hip up by holding your left knee and pulling it gently to the left. Then switch legs.

The Warrior Pose

Put your feet one-and-a-half leg lengths apart. Your right foot is at a ninety-degree angle, your left foot is at a forty-five-degree angle. Your heels are on the same line. Bend your right knee, trying to keep both hips open to the front (bottom photo). Engage

your quads. Your hands are parallel to the floor, your fingers are at shoulder height. Stare down your right middle finger. Hold for five strong breaths. Visualize how strong a curler you are.

Forward Fold Bend

Spread your feet one-and-a-half leg lengths apart. Fold over at your hips. Bring your hands down to the floor. Don't lock your knees, but keep them soft. Relax your head towards the floor. Walk your hands between your feet (below). This feels fabulous for my back and hamstring. Come up slowly, engaging your abs.

Congratulations, you've just finished the "Half-hour to Great Curling Workout."

During the off-season, I spend more time on other weights, I go to yoga classes, and I go for long bike rides. But when it's the middle of the season, this short and intense workout certainly keeps me game ready. Being fit helps to cut down on injuries and it means I don't tire on those three-game days.

THE HEAD GAME

I can't put a percentage on how much of curling is mental, but I do know this: I've played against many curlers with huge talent whose mental game got in the way. You need nerves of steel in this sport. It's extremely easy for negative thinking (that little inner voice that is busy saying can't, won't, don't) to rear its ugly head. If ever there was a sport for staying in the moment (while always mapping strategy out three and four shots ahead), it's curling.

When we won our first Tournament of Hearts in 1999 with a win over Cathy King, we were a bit naive. As defending champ, Cathy's team faced a lot more pressure. We were the underdog playing with nothing to lose, and we performed with the ease of low expectations. It was the last time we had the feeling. Once you win, expectations change and pressure grows. The key is to keep playing with the same innocence. In the Tournament of Hearts from 2001 to our dethroning in 2005 in St. John's, NL, we discovered first-hand what Cathy King would have known in 1999. It's hard to defend a title, to have a target on your back and other teams itching to beat you. All the pressure is on you to keep winning.

Once we won that championship in 1999, we were off to the world championship

The pressure facing a defending champion can be intense.

in Saint John, NB. The enormity of the event never hit us until we were eliminated. Sure, we knew we were going to a big event, but we had no benchmark of what the world championship would be like and no knowledge of the calibre of the other teams. I had competed at the worlds in 1982, but I knew that much had changed in those seventeen years. We didn't do our homework and really didn't even know what homework we should be doing. We were actually still in shock after winning the Canadian championship.

Predictably, then, we bombed at the worlds. Everything that could go wrong, did go wrong. Even the simplest of shots seemed hard. When Kim's back went out and she wound up totally immobile and in a wheelchair, we figured it was a sign from above that this tournament was going to be a learning experience for us. It was a tough loss; we had the dubious distinction of being the first Canadian team to miss the playoffs at the world championships and the media was rightfully hard on us. I went into a spiral of self-doubt that was difficult to get out of. So back at the Canadian championships in 2000, the questioning from the media began right away: "Are you guys really legit?" My confidence started to freefall.

Once that 2000 Canadian championship was over—and it was a disaster—we came to recognize this basic fact in one of our famous team meetings on Nancy's deck: we were good enough in terms of our shot-making, but too many times our heads got in the way, and it only takes one end of bad thinking to cause a loss. We realized we needed a sports psychologist. We had worked with sports psychologists in the past on a one-time basis, but we needed someone in our corner for the entire season. We found Ken Bagnell, who turned out to be a perfect fit for our team, although he is quick to point out that sports psychology isn't a magic bullet. "In order to win, sports psychology has to be developed in conjunction with all the other parts of the game, mainly your strategy and your shot-

COLLEEN'S SECRET

Things to Think About When Planning your Strategy:

1. **What's the score?**
2. **What's the end?**
3. **Who has the hammer?**
4. **How are you playing?**
5. **How is the other team playing?**
6. **What are the ice conditions like?**
7. **What's your gut telling you?**
8. **What shot do you know you can make?**

Learning not to dwell on bad shots is essential to becoming a top curler.

making," says Bagnell. "Right now, sports psychology is being used as a crutch. It's not a magic pill. You've got to do the work. At the elite level, everything you do will lead to that one percent edge and certainly mental training could add that one percent improvement, assuming you have the ninety-five percent of the whole package." These were Ken's wise words, but in my opinion, the advantage gained by becoming mentally tougher is far greater than one percent.

Certainly Ken was instrumental in our success, holding us accountable for everything. In the past we would cry about bad rocks, bad ice, the wrong time of day, that we didn't eat properly, that the other team made a lucky shot, and our favourite, that the curling gods were against us. We had many excuses for a loss, always avoiding the most obvious—that we missed too much or that maybe I called a bad end. Ken forced us to stop blaming everything else but ourselves for our losses. He made us take ownership of our performance. He also taught us to recognize when we were veering into negative talk and the absolute necessity

COLLEEN'S
SECRET

When coming up with a game plan, always be thinking three or four shots ahead. Think about what your opponent might call after you call your shot, and of course, always remember, it's not what you make, it's what you leave them.

of remaining positive about each other and whatever situation we found ourselves in. I'll never forget when we were in Gavle, Sweden, for the world championships. We thought the rocks were just awful and couldn't stop talking about them. We complained about the rocks for the first two days and Ken finally had it. He told us to cut it out. The rocks were the rocks—we had to deal with them and play them as best we could, but we had to stop the negative talk. I think he picked up on a crucial point: Sometimes in this game you have to deal with conditions that are less than ideal, but if you let them overwhelm you, you'll never win.

In order for a sports psychologist to be effective, you have to feel comfortable admitting your fears and phobias so the psychologist can help you work through them. You do need honesty in order to get the maximum benefit on the mental front, but don't kid yourself. Everyone gets a bit nervous before big games. Randy Ferbey, even after all he's done, told me, "I'm nervous before every game still. I might not show it, but I'm nervous. And do you know what? As soon as I lose that feeling, it's time to walk away from the game."

I think the biggest thing Ken helped me with was letting go. I had to learn to accept whatever happened and move on. In the past, when we'd have a nice end going and someone on our team would throw a rock behind the tee line, I would stew over the stupidity of it. When I went in the hack to throw my rock, all I could think about was someone else's missed shot—so then I would miss, too. This was something Ken had me work on through visualization and a lot of positive self-talk—my mantra became "it is what it is…deal with it."

Cal Botterill is one of the top sports psychologists in Canada. In addition to working with several of the top curling teams in Manitoba, he has worked at several Olympics with different Canadian athletes. He's excited that finally in the last decade curlers are embracing sports psychology.

But he warns that some teams are guilty of over-analysis. After watching and working with curlers, Botterill believes that the most underappreciated aspect of the sport is just how critical team support is. "How do you make a shot if your front end doesn't believe in you?" he asks. "You have to believe in one another completely. Curling at its best is an ego-less game where collective decisions have to be made." Botterill also thinks one of the most important parts of successful curling is controlling your reaction to misses:

No one has ever played a perfect game. No one. So if you respond well to mistakes you'll be golden. But it's so easy to take a miss, or a bad end, or a loss personally and overreact. But if you have learned how to prepare and have imagined it, if you start to learn how to see a solution for the next time things don't go exactly as planned, then you'll learn to handle mistakes better. At the top level, all the players know they'll make mistakes; they are a part of the game. It's seeing a solution for the next time that's so important. You'll often hear coaches tell players something like, "the team that makes the fewest mistakes will win." I like to rephrase that to, "it's the team who reacts and responds best to all the challenges in the course of the game who'll win."

Botterill says the best recipe for winning is simple: "Trust your shot and preparation and perform." Easy to say, easier to do with a lot of practice.

Another sports psychologist I've worked with is Paul Dennis from the Toronto Maple Leafs. He introduced me to the concept of "ironic processing theory." Here's how it works: when an athlete focusses excessively on a negative thought, even if their focus is on avoiding a potentially negative situation, the negative situation or performance the athlete is trying to avoid becomes more likely to occur. Dennis uses the example of a professional golfer to illustrate the theory:

> Let's assume a golfer needs to clear a large body of water to land his shot on the green. If he obsesses about "I must avoid the water," it's not uncommon for the ball to wind up in the water. This is an example of the ironic processing theory—it's ironic that the very thing you are trying to avoid is front and centre in your consciousness.

Dennis told me this often happens when an athlete feels stress. As you might expect, concentration on the task at hand is important:

> The athlete needs to focus on breathing, relax, and focus on the task. So the golfer should focus on

Visualize yourself making the perfect shot beforehand. Then do it.

the pin on the green and not the water. A curler should focus on the technique needed for the shot and should not worry about what could go wrong because of the obstacles in the way. As soon as our thoughts drift to obstacles that might impact on a negative result, the probability of the negative result increases. Our mindset is a powerful tool. It must be positive and proactive, not fearful and tentative.

This makes perfect sense to me. I can't tell you how many times I've missed a shot where the last thought in my head was "don't hit the guard." The next thing I knew, I was crashing all over the guard. Another example is when I might say to myself, "Don't be deep here," and sure enough I'll slide behind the tee line. This is ironic processing theory at work. So make sure the thoughts going on in your head are positive. Visualize yourself making the shot perfectly. Take a deep breath—and throw it perfectly!

**Consider your options carefully, then focus on the shot at hand.
Always trust your own abilities.**

THE ELEVEN C'S OF CURLING

When I was a kid I memorized Ken Watson's seven c's of curling: compatibility, concentration, cooperation, courage, confidence, competitiveness, and consistency. All of these still hold true, but I have four more for the list—chemistry, commitment, communication, and calm. Let's go through the list.

Compatibility: There are many talented curlers who don't win because they don't get along. When putting together a team, look for the right fit of personalities as well as people who love their positions and will support each other through thick and thin.

Concentration: You have to focus on your game and not what's happening on the next sheet. Focus on the shot you're playing right now, not what you missed last end or what might happen two shots from now. In an arena, there's the distraction of the crowd, television cameras, and officials. Practice your focus and concentration every time you step on the ice at your club when you are out throwing. If something is happening on the next sheet, work on blocking it out.

Cooperation: Curling is a team game and anytime you're a cog in the wheel of a team, you have to work together in order to have success.

Cooperation is one of the keys to curling success.

COLLEEN'S
SECRET

It's not enough just to make shots. In order to win you need the complete package. So after every game, do a mental checklist of how many of the eleven c's you excelled at and which areas you need to work on. Make yourself a complete player. (Maybe we've just made it the twelve c's of curling.)

Courage: When the game is on the line, you'll need lots of courage. Curling is a sport that definitely requires nerves of steel. You need to be fearless, so show courage when times look tough.

Confidence: Obviously confidence is a huge ingredient to winning. You've got to believe in yourself and your teammates in order to have any success in this sport. But confidence is a fragile thing, because this

Communication between teammates should always be positive.

sport can be very humbling. A few missed shots are enough to shatter confidence. Stay positive and keep believing.

Competitiveness: This is the hunger, that drive, that pushes a team to greatness. I always thought I hated losing more than I liked winning. I was driven to find ways to keep getting a little bit better.

Consistency: The ability to make the same shots over and over is crucial to

COLLEEN'S SECRET

In addition to the eleven c's of curling, there are the six p's of curling:

perfect
practice prevents
piss-poor
performance.

success. Whether it's above the tee line for draw weight or nailing those hits, certain shots have to be automatic in order to win. I know I was lucky to have three of the most consistent players in front of me. They made all the simple shots, so there were never any hard shots for me. Nancy, Mary-Anne, and Kim were perennial all-stars and almost always tops in scoring statistics at their positions.

Chemistry: Chemistry is really an intangible, but every winning team has it. You can't buy it, you can't manufacture it, but when it's there, it's golden, and it certainly is a trademark of all winning teams. If you are always dreading going to the rink, if curling is just no fun, or if someone's always bickering about something or someone, these are good signs that your chemistry is a bit off.

Commitment: It takes a lot of energy, desire, and hard work to win and all four people on the team have to be equally committed. If someone on your team is

already booking a ski holiday just before your playdowns, that's an indication that the commitment level isn't what it should be. There's another kind of commitment too, and that's commitment to the strategy and the shot that is being called. Don't expect to make a shot the team isn't committed to.

Communication: Again, communication between teammates is

COLLEEN'S SECRET

When coming up with your game plan, be realistic about your ability. Are you comfortable drawing to the pin against three in the second end? I never was—I'm a slow starter. Are you comfortable drawing to the pin against three of your opponent's rocks in the seventh end? I was. Funny thing—same shot, just at different stages of the game. I was more comfortable once the ice was worked in; heavy curling club ice in the opening two ends was my nemesis. I carried this over to arenas even though the ice there starts out in fine condition and sometimes becomes a little suspect down the stretch.

critical. Knowing when to talk and what to say in a pressure situation is important. Skips have to be willing to listen and open-minded to the input from their teammates, and conversely, team members have to realize when they are talking too much and giving too much information to the skip. Communicate in a positive manner. If I was coming down to draw around the guard, Kim and Mary-Anne would give me the time and tell me they'd get it there for me. This was great communication—much better than saying "don't be deep" or "don't hit the guard."

Calm: Find your zen. If you panic in this game, if you don't control your nerves, you might as well get used to that "also ran" status. Breathe. Relax. It is only a game after all.

COLLEEN'S SECRET

It was only when we came up with a team strategy that we started to dominate. We sat down with Gerry Peckham from the CCA with a big chart and a marker and went over different scenarios, honestly discussing what we thought we could make in every situation. While coming up with our plan, we had to consider our lack of a really big-weight, run-back shot that the men have (by big weight, I mean in the six-second range). Once we went through all the scenarios, our plan became more obvious.

THE KISS STRATEGY

To say I've used the Keep It Simple Strategy (KISS) over my career would be an understatement. The four-rock rule, which doesn't allow you to hit rocks between the house and hog line until four rocks have been played, means there are a lot of possibilities for how to generate offence, making it even tougher to play defence. The bottom line is still the same as when I first started curling—when you have last rock you want to score two or more, and when you don't, you want to hold the opposition to one. Don't let them steal. If you look at the stats from past Tournament of Hearts and Briers, the team that allowed the fewest steals was almost always the team that won. Of course, this strategy is easier said than done, but knowing when to bail out of an end is important.

Our simple strategy flew in the face of conventional wisdom, yet it allowed us to win five Canadian women's titles. But we were the Rodney Dangerfield of women's curling—we didn't get a lot of respect because we wouldn't play the traditional approach of flat-out offence. Our strategy made the most efficient use of our resources at each position to provide us with our best chance of winning. I knew I didn't have the ability to throw a cross-house double

Perfect execution of simple shots became our team's calling card.

take-out like the great Kevin Martin, nor could I do the fancy run backs like Brad Gushue. My strength lay in my ability to consistently make simple shots, and only every now and then pull out some razzle-dazzle. My team bought into the game plan and executed beautifully, so our games often came down to high drama in the ninth and tenth ends. That became our calling card. While many criticized our

Interesting Stats

If you look at the statistics for the last few Scotties and Briers, the eventual winners all average around eight points a win, while holding their opponents to 5.5 points or less. In our 2004 win in Red Deer, we averaged 8.2 points per game, while holding our opponents to 5.5. Just to compare, at the 2007 Scotties, Kelly Scott scored 8.1 points and held her opponents to a lowly 4.2 points per game. Glenn Howard at the 2007 Brier averaged 8.2 points per game while holding his opponents to 4.7 points per game.

The Need to Steal

At the 2004 Scotties Tournament of Hearts in Red Deer, we stole twenty-three ends, while only seven were stolen against us. At the 2007 Scotties, Kelly Scott, who successfully defended her title, stole nineteen ends and only five ends were stolen on her. And at the 2007 Brier, Glenn Howard stole twenty ends and only eight ends were stolen on him. Don't allow yourself to lose in the stealing department.

simplicity, we never bent to those critics who felt the game should be played a certain way. We just found a strategy that worked for our team and perfected it. It's no different than watching Jacques Lemaire's neutral zone trap in hockey. Television executives might not like it, but it won him a couple of Stanley Cups with the New Jersey Devils. We simply found a strategy that we thought we could be successful with—and we ran with it.

There seems to me to be a cookie-cutter approach to strategy these days. The team throwing first is throwing red, and throws it top four. The other skip, throwing yellow and with hammer, throws a corner guard. Now red guards. Yellow comes around and makes a corner freeze, red tries a corner freeze, yellow tries a tap or a big run back—you get the picture. All of sudden you need your million-dollar shot to get out of the end.

When you're watching games on television, keep in mind a few things. You're not Glenn Howard. Great players have the ability to make six-second run backs or doubles to get themselves out of a jam, and they are playing on some of the best ice going with great rocks—way better then the club ice you'll be playing your provincial championship on. You might want to start with something a little simpler. Someday you will be as great as Howard, Gushue, and Stoughton. But take baby steps; you've got to learn to crawl before you can walk. Play with a strategy that keeps you at your comfort level. Chart what you did after your game.

What worked? What didn't?

I've had long strategy sessions with Russ Howard, Rick Folk, and Randy Ferbey. When Mark Dacey is practising beside me I often pick his brain about different scenarios. No one uses the exact same strategy, so it's best to try several different methods yourself and see what works for you and your team instead of just copying what you see on television. Sure, there are tried-and-true curling laws, but experiment and chart the results. One thing that I always had to take into consideration when I consulted the top skips was their ability to throw big heat (six seconds between the hogs). That allowed for some impressive cleaning up in an end. Plus, the male sweepers can generally hold line better (keep a shot straighter) than even my strong sweepers. In my mind, Mary-Anne Arsenault is one of the best women throwers, and especially good at big-weight shots. But even the best Mary-Anne could muster was 7.5-second weight, and while that's impressive, it's not with the same power that men throw.

One thing my team did for a three-year period to try to improve was to play only in

COLLEEN'S SECRET

There are two systems of time clocks, both designed to speed up play and prevent curlers from being too slow with their decisions. At provincial and Canadian championships, the total time allowed per team is seventy-five minutes. The clock operates like a chess clock...it's turned off when the skip surrenders the house and the sweepers clear off to the side of the sheet. Then the other team's clocks starts. On the World Curling Tour, they use what's called "thinking time"—each team has thirty-five minutes, and the clock only runs when the skip is making the call and debating what to do. The clock is stopped when the thrower is throwing (unlike at provincial and Canadian championships, where it continues to run as long as your team is using the ice). I usually "bank" time early on by playing a quick and open style. I do this because I know in the later ends I'll need a little more time to think about strategy when things get more complicated.

men's cashspiels. This was a real eye-opener for us. It clearly showed us what a gap there is between the men's and women's game, and that difference was, you guessed it, in the big-weight shots. We'd have a nice end set up and be thinking we'd score a deuce only to

have our plans dashed by a spectacular big-weight shot. While that part was frustrating, I think playing the men improved our game overall. We knew we had to make great shots end after end in order to compete with them.

When thinking of your strategy, think of a game like a good book. There's a beginning, middle, and end in every story. You don't necessarily need to uncover the plot in the first two chapters. The same is true in curling. I look at the first two ends as a time for testing the ice. I do this for two reasons. I've been burned too many times by ice changes, especially in arena conditions. Often the ice can be a little faster and straighter once you get to the playoffs. Plus, when I'm playing under a time limit, I can bank some time by playing the first two ends quickly. From the third to seventh ends, it's moving time. But I'm only trying to make a move when I have last rock. When the other team has hammer, they'll have to go hard on offence because I'll be hitting everything

COLLEEN'S
SECRET

When coming up with a game plan, it's important to consider ice conditions, who has last rock, the score, the end you're in, how you're playing, and how your opponent is playing. In 2001 when we were playing in the Canadian women's final, we were in an extra end against Kelly Law with last rock. While some experts probably felt I should have called for a draw to the four-foot for the win, I instead played a tough out-turn hit and roll. My reasoning? Draw weight had changed drastically during the course of the game. I would have just been guessing at what to throw. So I played the hit and roll and the outcome came down to a measurement. It was the longest measurement of my life. If we won the measurement, the Canadian title was ours. It seemed to take forever—but we won by a few millimetres.

Diagram 8.1

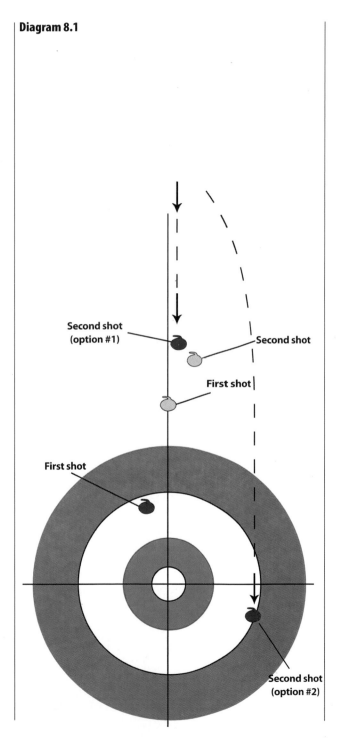

Second shot (option #1)

Second shot

First shot

First shot

Second shot (option #2)

I see. I try hard to get my opponent to score in the seventh, because I want hammer in the eighth and the all-important tenth end. So, of course, like a chess game, you're not only thinking several shots ahead in every end, but you're plotting how to navigate your way into having last rock when it matters most—the final end.

But enough theory. Let's look at a few situations curlers often find themselves in.

You are tied in the last end and have last rock (the other team is throwing yellow rocks and you're throwing red rocks). They throw a guard (diagram 8.1). You can either play a chip (option #1) or come around top eight (option #2). Let two things be your guide when you are deciding to chip or not. First, is this a shot your lead regularly makes? Second, are the ice conditions working for the chip? If you aren't going to chip, you play the come-around. It's critical, of course, that your lead throw it top eight and ideally we always wanted this rock well exposed, even fully open. We found leaving the rock exposed tempted the other team to play full tap weight on it and push it to back eight as opposed to a straight freeze, which would be tougher for us to remove. If the other skip wisely elects to throw a second centre guard instead, and if the ice allows for it, then we would throw a chip since, in a tie game, we don't want the house to get too crowded. While the chip is a first option, if the ice isn't good for chipping, you have two options: come around and freeze to your first rock, or draw to the open side. If you draw to the open side, it must be deep enough not to allow your opponent to play an in-off later in the end. The rest of the end is pretty obvious—we go into peeling mode. If a peel is missed, you're back to weighing your options.

We used to play two chips with the lead's first rocks religiously, but after analyzing what really worked for us, we came up with the "get in first" strategy and then chipped with our second rock. We arrived at the decision simply based on results. While Nancy was really good at the chip shot, she was only human. She probably made it seventy-five percent of the time. Nancy's come-around-top-eight shot, however, was a shot she nailed probably ninety-five percent of the time. So we went with execution.

Let's move onto the one-down scenario

COLLEEN'S SECRET

When devising your team's game plan, play to your team's strength. We were an out-turn team. When we won the 1999 Scott Tournament of Hearts, we threw 611 out-turns, and 396 in-turns. In 2004, nothing much changed. We threw 658 out-turns to 311 in-turns. Know your strengths and milk them for all you can.

where you have last rock (assume you're throwing red again). There are many ways to play this end and I'm going to throw out a number of possibilities. First, you have to decide whether you're going to be cautious or aggressive about scoring your deuce for the win.

Let's suppose yellow throws it top four with their opening shot. You can play a corner guard, you can freeze, you can tap it back twelve, or you can hit and roll to the wings and then freeze to it after they nose hit it (diagrams 8.2a, b, c, d). I've seen Jennifer Jones's rink always throw the corner guard with no hesitation. I've seen Kelly Scott's team play a lot of the tap backs and

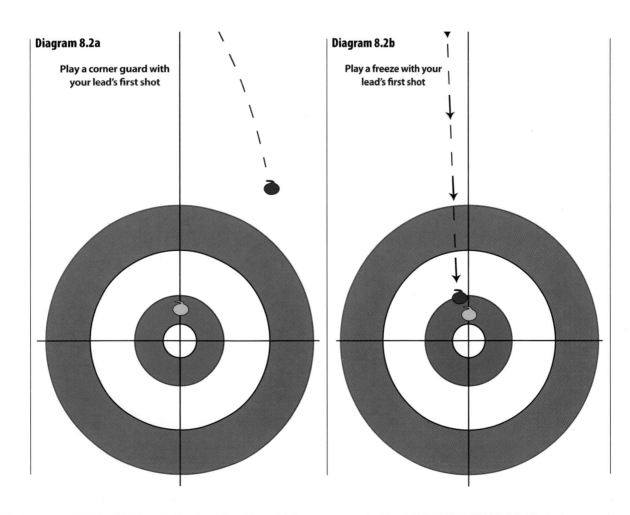

Diagram 8.2a

Play a corner guard with your lead's first shot

Diagram 8.2b

Play a freeze with your lead's first shot

eventually they lock on for the freeze. And I've seen our team play the hit and roll out of the four-foot to the wings and throw the corner guard on the second shot.

Here's where you have to do an assessment of the ice and your opponent. Think of the shots the other team has made and missed. Also consider how the ice is holding up. When mapping out the strategy in any end, these are two important things to factor in, along with the obvious—what has been the strength of your team in this particular game, under these ice conditions? In the course of an end there are often two

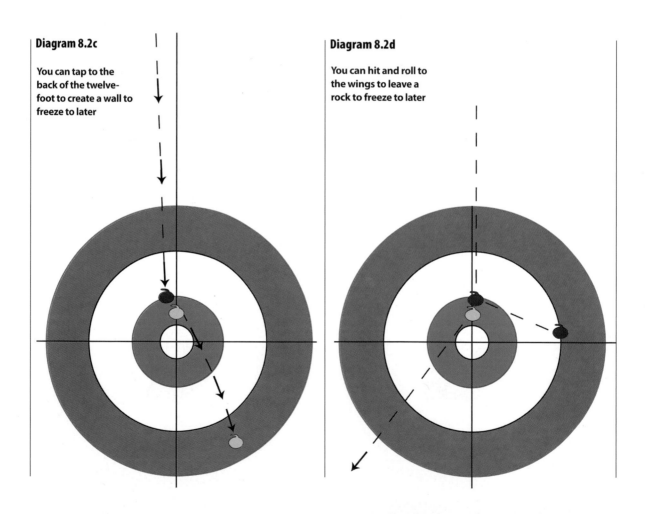

Diagram 8.2c

You can tap to the back of the twelve-foot to create a wall to freeze to later

Diagram 8.2d

You can hit and roll to the wings to leave a rock to freeze to later

Remember: it's not what you make, it's what you leave them.

In this photo, Colleen Jones and Jennifer Jones consider their options

at the 2006 Olympic curling trials.

The 2001 Tournament of Hearts win came down to a dramatic measurement in the final end, a measurement which ended up in our favour.

or three good options on every shot—weigh them all and choose the smartest for your team and for the ice conditions.

Let's stay with the one-down scenario and you have last rock. Your opponents decide to play hard for the steal and they throw their first rock short.

Again, there are several options for your first rock. You can come around right away or you can throw a corner guard. Another crazy option is to draw deep to the open side. What do you suppose your opponent will do with that rock? Will they ignore it and put up a second guard? Will they ignore it and draw around the guard? Or will they hit the open rock? This is where the cat-and-mouse game gets interesting and this is where great execution is vital.

Remember: it's not what you make, but what you leave. This should always be in the back of your mind when you're calling shots. In round-robin play at the 2007 Brier, Newfoundland's Brad Gushue was playing British Columbia's Dean Joannise. British Columbia was up by two, sitting shot rock in the four-foot. Newfoundland was sitting number two and three in front of the shot rock, but at a terrible angle that wouldn't have allowed Gushue any angle for running it back.

With his last rock Joannise opted to play a double. If he had thrown a guard or even thrown it away, Gushue wouldn't have had a shot for the tie. But he opted to play the double, wound up chipping one out, and left Gushue in great shape for the tap out for two, which he made. Before he went to throw his ill-advised double, Joannise should have taken some time to think about the situation.

Gushue wound up stealing the extra end for the win.

One other thing to consider during the middle ends of the game is this: don't panic. Often, we score a two to go up 3–1 after four ends, and the other team plays such hard offence to score their deuce that we wind up

COLLEEN'S SECRET

Reading the ice is a big part of your strategy. I asked Randy Ferbey for his best advice on reading ice and he laughed and said his team would laugh, too. "I don't watch the ice very closely. I especially don't watch the other teams. Skips tend to get caught up in what their opponent is doing. Well, they might have throwing tendencies that you don't know about. You have to [play] according to your team's delivery and ice. Dave [Nedohin] and I know we can take less ice on our out-turns because they're going to run straight. So reading ice isn't an art, but reading your team's delivery and releases is the key."

COLLEEN'S
SECRET

The question I've been asked the most is whether I would rather be up one coming home without hammer, or down one with. Hands down, I'd take being down one with hammer. To me, that feels like full control of an end. When you're one up without the last rock, you have to make the decision to try to steal or force the opposition to one. Both are acceptable strategies, but be prepared to execute well, because one little mistake and, as a rule, it's game over.

stealing. Remember what your grandma told you: patience is a virtue.

Another buzz phrase in curling strategy is "risk versus reward." As a skip, you may sometimes call a tough shot because the payoff is huge if it's made—a tough run back, for example, that will give you a three and crack the game open. There is certainly much to consider when deciding what shot to play. The most important thing is to calculate

objectively what the odds are of making the tougher shot. Remember the statistic that has been proven over and over again at both the Canadian men's and women's championships: the team holding the trophy at the end of the event always allowed the fewest steals. If you have a moment of doubt over the shot, definitely don't call it, and if you think realistically the chances of making it are less than fifty-fifty, just play a simple draw.

I can't tell you how many times my team has thrown our game plan out the window and just gone with our gut. (That was one of Nancy's favourite lines when we were unsure what to play. She'd ask, "What's your gut telling you?") Trust your instincts on a shot; those hunches are fairly reliable.

Even though our strategy was incredibly simple, it required great execution. For example, if our opponents threw their first rock top four, our move with Nancy was to hit and roll to the twelve-foot. Usually our opponents would nose hit and Nancy would throw to the corner with her second rock. Now our opponents would often be scratching their heads. Do they choke the corner guard, peel it, or throw it side four-foot? Whatever they chose as their next shot, we felt like we were casting our net and would have an opportunity to reel in our deuce. But it did require terrific execution of simple shots. If they chose to peel the corner guard, we would keep throwing the corner guard for a couple more shots, knowing we could always freeze to the rock in the wings. If we were playing a great peeling team, this plan of attack wasn't going to be effective, but if we'd scouted our opponent and realized peeling was not their forte (often a reality in the women's game), this plan of attack led to more than a few deuces for us.

I'm going to give you a few scenarios from different games over the years. Think about how you would approach these if you were making the call. Remember that great strategy is dependent on great execution. You can map out an end perfectly, but if the shots aren't made, it's all for naught.

COLLEEN'S SECRET

To reiterate our team strategy, we'd talk to each other after every end. We'd quickly go over what we wanted to happen in the next end. If we had a big lead, we'd just say, "get your peeling boots on." If we were tied in the eighth end, we'd talk about the importance of making sure we scored, preferably a deuce, although the object in this scenario was just to make sure we scored. Of course we would throw a blank if the opportunity arose in the eighth, but we would most likely be looking to score, hold them to one in the ninth end, and have last rock coming home. Whatever game plan your team comes up with, talk it over and make sure everyone's on board.

Scenario #1: Risk vs. Reward

Game: Brier final 2007—Brad Gushue versus Glenn Howard

Score: 5–5

End: seventh

Hammer: Gushue

Decision Time: If you're Gushue, do you draw for one to go up one going into the eighth, or do you play the tough double for three to take control?

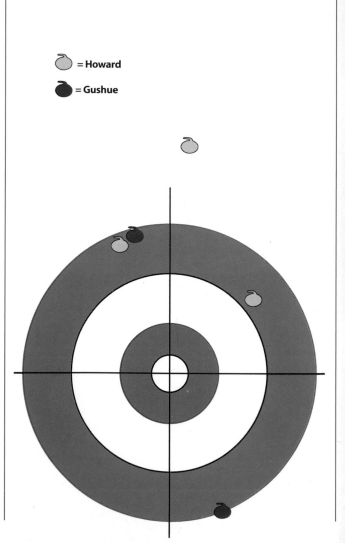

= Howard

= Gushue

How to Play It: Gushue attempts a tough, thin double. It is a tough shot, but it is awfully tempting. He must hit his Newfoundland rock to remove the first Ontario rock, then his shooter must scoot over and remove the second Ontario rock. Making it perfectly would score Gushue three, and he was probably thinking that in the worst-case scenario, he'd remove one Ontario rock and give up a steal of one. But disaster strikes when Gushue hits the guard, giving Ontario a steal of two for a 7–5 lead with three ends to play. Gushue felt his last rock picked; Ontario thought he just threw it tight. Regardless, the debate remains, should he have drawn for one, or was this the right shot to call?

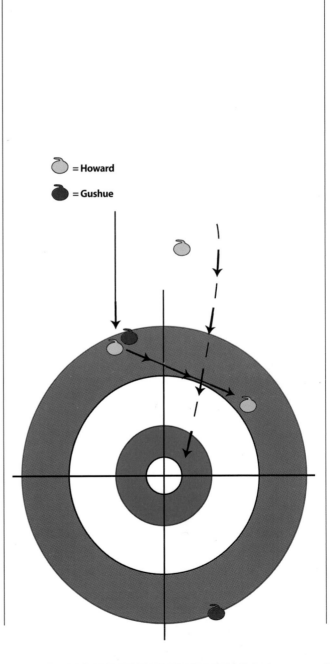

= Howard
= Gushue

Scenario #2:

Play it Safe or Go For Broke

Game: Tournament of Hearts 2007 semifinal—Jennifer Jones versus Kelly Scott

Score: 2–0 Scott

End: second

Hammer: Jones

Decision Time: Jennifer has to choose between a draw for one, or the tougher in-off for two to tie the game up.

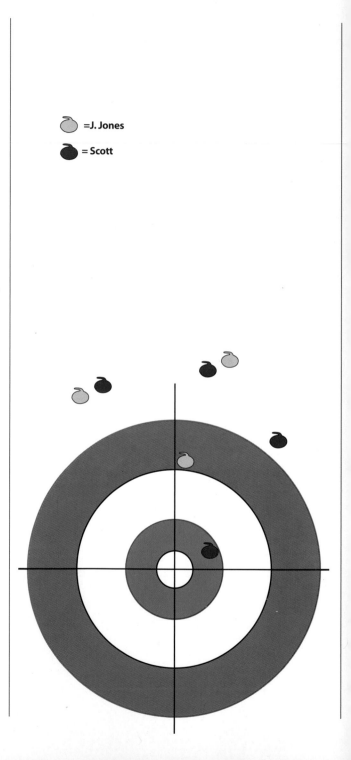

How to Play It: Sometimes when you get down by two early in the game, you become overly anxious to tie the game as quickly as possible. In this situation, Jones could draw full four-foot for one or play the much tougher in-off, try to remove the Scott rock in the four foot, and stay for two.

The latter is a shot Jones loves to play and often makes, but there is no question it's a harder shot than the draw for one. Jones tries the more difficult shot and hits the rock at the edge of the rings too thick—she catches a bit of Scott's rock, but not enough. Scott steals one for a 3–0 lead. What would you have played?

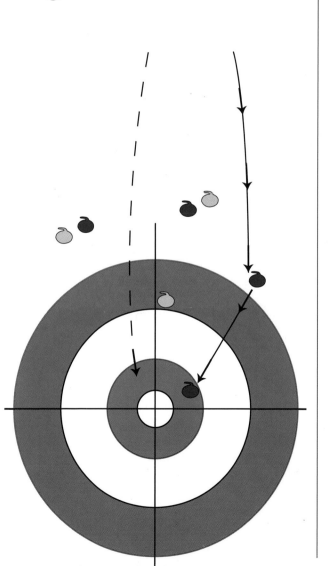

Scenario #3: Late-End Drama

Game: 2007 Canada Cup final—

Cathy King versus Jennifer Jones

Score: 7–7

End: ninth

Hammer: King

Decision Time: Do you want to score a

multiple point end or blank? It's important to

decide early.

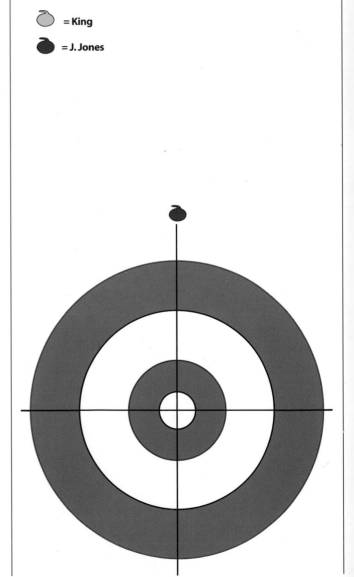

How to Play It: This is such an

interesting situation and one you'll find

yourself in a million times. You're tied in

the ninth end and you have last rock. You

have to decide whether you're looking to

score two or leave the end blank in order to

have last rock coming home. When I'm in

this situation, the last thing I want to have

happen is for us to score one and I really

don't want to give up a steal. In this scenario

you have to assess what the opposition is

going to give you after the first rock of the

end. If their lead throws top four, I'm going for the blank every time. If their lead throws a halfway guard, I'm going around. If the lead throws a really tight guard—they've got me thinking. In Cathy's final game against Jennifer at the Canada Cup, Jennifer's lead threw a tight guard, inches from the rings.

Cathy drew around and her lead was perfect top four. On the surface it looked golden, but it led to a heap of trouble and by the time the end was over, Cathy was facing three Jones rocks and wound up allowing a steal of one. I would suggest that Cathy had two options other than the straight come-around. The first, given the guard rock was so tight, was to play a chip; the second option was to draw to the open side. If she had played either of these shots, what do you suppose Jennifer's next move would have been?

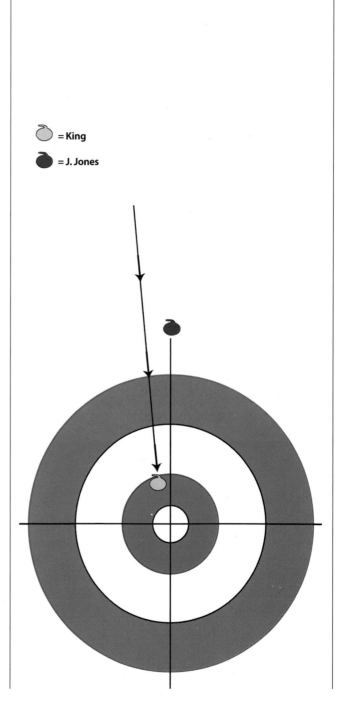

Scenario #4: Another Way to Steal

Game: 2007 Canada Cup final—
Kevin Martin versus Randy Ferbey

Score: 8–8

End: eleventh

Hammer: Ferbey

Decision Time: Not a lot of decisions in this scenario—Ferbey has to score one to win!

= Martin

= Ferbey

How to Play It: The traditional approach for stealing the end is simple. Put up a centre guard, hope the other team doesn't chip it away, and then bury a rock behind it. As expected, Martin's first lead rock is a tight guard. Ferbey calls a chip, and it's made perfectly by all-star lead Marcel Rocque, with both rocks rolling into the twelve-foot. Martin calls another guard, and Rocque again chips this one, this time over to the side boards—a beautiful shot. It was decision time for Martin. Tradition says to throw another centre guard, but Martin called a come-around on the Ferbey rock

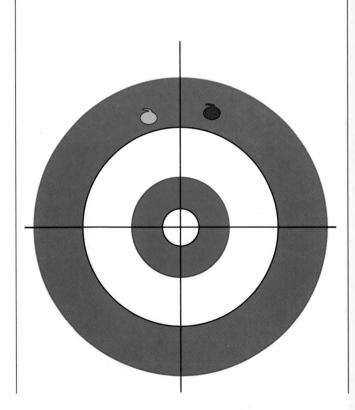

that was top twelve. Martin's second drew to the back eight-foot. I love Martin's call and I've included it here for you to talk over with your team. How do you go about stealing after your opposition has made two good chip shots? This was a good strategy that Martin came up with, and chances are he'll be returning to the out-front guard strategy with his second's next shot.

Your overall goal is that your opponent peels out the end and with your skip's last rock, you'll put it in the eight-foot, making the opposing skip draw against two with his last rock. How this end played out was less than textbook because there were a couple of less than perfect executions from Martin and his third, John Morris. Ferbey, with Dave Nedohin throwing skip rocks, drew to Martin's rock in the back of the four-foot for the win. However, I drew it up for you to look at other ways of stealing after the opposition has made a chip shot.

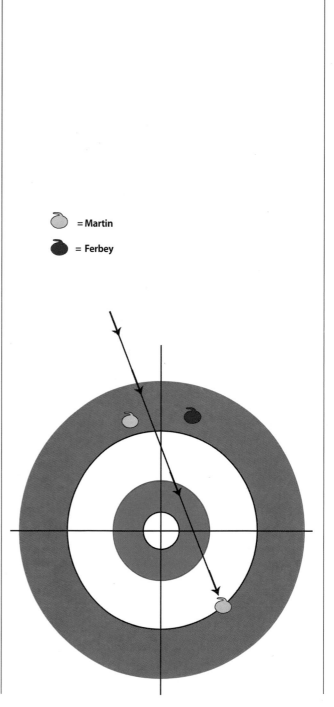

= Martin

= Ferbey

PUTTING IT ALL TOGETHER

With the World Curling Tour making the switch to games of eight ends, it probably won't be long for ten-end games to go the way of the dinosaur. This change will be a major advantage for teams who are good at getting off to fast starts. A two-point lead early in an eight-end game can look insurmountable if you're the team playing from behind. But no matter what changes come to the game, that old mantra in curling still rings true: Hold your opponent to one when they have last rock, score your deuce when you have hammer.

The other change to the game has accompanied curling's inclusion at the Olympics. The Olympics' importance means the emphasis in this country has shifted away from the Canadian championship. Now curlers have Olympic ambitions, and we are already seeing the trend towards assembling teams based on talent and not geography, as was traditional. For this to work, you need to find people who work well independently. Curling has always been a sport that requires hours of team practice, playing in your club super league, and provincial play. However, many other Olympic teams, like the women's hockey team, for example, get together for training camp and the team is selected based strictly on ability. I really believe this is the future of curling, and it's a future I'm looking forward to.

In my decades of playing the game, I've been lucky to curl against some of curling's great players. From my childhood idol, Lindsay Sparkes, to some of the great women's teams skipped by legends like Connie Laliberte, Marilyn Bodough, Cathy King, Kelly Scott, Kelley Law, Jennifer Jones, and of course, the greatest of them all, Sandra Schmirler. Every time I stepped onto the ice against them, I tried to learn a little bit more about the game, how they played it, and what their on-ice demeanour was. I am constantly learning and marvel at all the subtle nuances in the sport. I hope some of the things I've learned help your game and I hope you get just a fraction of the joy I've received from the "grand old game."

My good friend, Jim Waite, national coach for the Canadian men's squad, has watched more great curling than probably any person on the planet. He's been to fifteen world championships and three Olympic Games and we won't bother counting all the Canadian championships, Ontario provincial championships, and cashspiels he's been to. I asked him what the difference usually is between the winning team and the others in the field. He said it's different every time, but one constant is that the winning team "plays with no fear." He used the last three world championships as an example. "Glenn Howard's team won the 2007 worlds and from the very start, the team was so exceptional there was little doubt about the outcome. But all teams aren't like that. Jean-Michel Ménard's team, who represented Canada in 2006, was different because they won the silver and that was amazing when you consider how little international experience they had. Randy Ferbey's team in 2005 in Victoria didn't really have their game there, but they still found a way to win and they did it in so many different ways."

Putting together a winning team is like following a good recipe—you need a little of that, a little of this, stir it all together, bake it

**Building a winning team isn't easy, but the payoff
is well worth the effort.**

at just the right temperature, and voila. But let's go over the ingredients one last time. You need four good throwers with a lot of passion who also get along. You need to practise and bonspiel in order to learn and get better—it doesn't happen on its own. You need to take feedback about your game, process it, and make the necessary changes. You need to have a game plan and a strategy that works for you. You need to have mental toughness that will serve you well when you get in those championship games at the club level, or at provincial, Canadian, or world championships. But you will need all of the components together to make a great, winning team—so get working and good curling.

CURLING GLOSSARY

Backline:

The line at the back of the ice. Rocks that cross this line are out of play.

Button:

The circle at the centre of the house, two feet in diameter.

Chip:

A shot played by the lead. The lead tries to "chip" a front guard over to the boards without removing it from play.

Draw:

When a curler delivers the rock slowly enough that the rock winds up in the house or out in front as a guard.

End:

Like an inning in baseball for curlers. Curlers play either eight- or ten-end games. An end is over after all eight rocks from the two teams have been thrown. A blank end occurs when neither team scores a point.

Four-rock rule:

The rule that states no opponent's rocks can be removed from play until at least four rocks (total) have been thrown.

Freeze:

When you draw perfectly in front of another stone.

Guard:

The term describing the rocks that sit in front of the house and protect other rocks already in the house.

Hack:

The piece of rubber from which curlers deliver rocks. Right-handed curlers throw from the left hack and left-handed curlers use the right hack.

Hammer:

The last rock in a curling end.

Hard:

The universal command yelled at sweepers. You'll also hear "right off," which means the sweepers should leave the rock alone.

Hit:

A rock delivered with enough weight to remove an opponent's rock from play.

Hog:

A rock that doesn't make it over the far hog line. Such a rock is called a hogged rock and must be removed from play while the thrower hides his or her head in shame. There are two hog lines, one at each end of the sheet, ten metres in front of the hack. Curlers must release their rocks before the first hog line, and the rock must cross the second hog line to be in play. The penalty for either offence is having the stone removed from play.

House:

The series of rings curlers aim their rocks toward. There are two houses on each sheet. The circles, or rings, consist of the twelve-foot circle on the outside, the eight-foot in the middle, and the four-foot on the inside, the smallest ring. The small, solid circle in the very middle that looks like a bull's eye is the button.

In-off:

A type of shot where curlers roll a rock "in" the house, "off" another rock (usually in the wings).

In-turn and out-turn:

To make a rock curl, curlers put a slight turn on the rock at the point of release. Using the face of a clock as a reference, for an in-turn, curlers start the handle at about ten o'clock and release it at about twelve o'clock. An in-turn will turn clockwise down the ice. For an out-turn, curlers start it at two o'clock and release it at about twelve o'clock (the opposite for left-handed throwers). Out-turns spin in a counter-clockwise direction.

Narrow:

It means the thrower was on the tight side of the broom. Conversely, if a thrower was wide, it means he or she was on the fat side of the broom. Either way, the thrower didn't throw it the way the skip wanted, which is right up the broom.

Pebble:

The fine spray of water that covers the ice before play begins. The spray creates tiny bumps ("pebbles") on the surface of the ice.

Peel:

A hard take-out, normally used to remove guards from play.

Pick:

A rock that changes direction after "picking" up something on the ice.

Raise:

When a curler plays their rock onto another. Either a draw raise or a raise run back can remove an opponent's rock from play.

Rock:

A forty-two-pound hunk of polished granite that curlers throw down the ice. Also called a stone.

Sheet:

The ice on which curlers play.

Skip:

The person who throws the last two rocks of an end and calls the game. The third is the curler on the team who throws the third pair of rocks and holds the broom while the skip is throwing. These two positions are called the back end. The front end is made up of the second, who throws the second two rocks of the end, and the lead, who throws the first pair.

Take-out:

Removing another rock from play by hitting it with another rock. Same as a hit.

Tee line:

The line that intersects the house, parallel to the hog lines.

Weight:

The amount of force curlers use to throw a rock, usually measure in time or by the rock's final resting place. For example:

Peel weight would be big weight for the rock to hit and roll away.

Hack weight is enough weight to push the rock to the hack.

Backline weight is enough to push the opponent's rock to the backline.

Guard weight is enough weight to stop outside the house.

Wings:

The edge of the sheet of ice or the outer edges of the house.

ACKNOWLEDGEMENTS

So many people have had a hand in helping me along the journey. My parents' lack of curling knowledge, combined with low expectations, kept the pressure off as a kid. My father always said, "you can't possibly win"; my mother always said, "just do your best." In hindsight, it was great parental advice, though goodness knows I was always determined to prove Dad wrong!

My sisters were instrumental in those early years. They gave me someone to practice with and to use as a sounding board—especially Barbara and Monica—and I always had a guaranteed team, too! I can't thank them enough for all their support.

The late Hughie Little, an old-timer at the club, used to play me up and back for a dollar when I was a kid. I looked forward to, and learned a lot from, our games of one-on-one. Joyce Myers spent endless hours with many of the Jones kids, coaching us in curling and in life, and I know that every lucky break I've had on the ice are those two angels—Hughie and Joyce—watching out for me.

Peter Corkum was instrumental to our team's success and we could always feel his belief in us. Rick Folk spent two years consulting with us and I learned so much listening to the master (I just wish I could draw like him). Gerry Peckham from the Canadian Curling Association took many phone calls and spent many hours on the ice with me. Even though I was probably nagging him, he never made me feel that way, and I always knew he'd have a solution to whatever it was that wasn't working for me. I always liked his long pause followed by, "Hmm…why don't you try…"

Laine Peters and Mary Sue Radford, our two fifth players and unsung heroes, really deserve a whole chapter in this book. Their insight into our games and the energy they brought to the team was priceless—and Mary Sue's sarcastic sense of humour always made me laugh no matter what the situation.

Ken Bagnell, our long-time coach, probably spent many hours wondering what he got himself into with our crazy gang. We never would have won without him…a great coach and friend.

Nancy, Kim, and Mary-Anne were just the best curling teammates a skip could ever ask for and we enjoyed our ride together… and what a ride!

To the fans who said we gave them heart attacks, tears of joy, and tears of sadness— thank you for your kind letters and emails over the years.

And to Scott, Zach, and Luke—I'm the luckiest gal in the world to have you three!